SOCCER'S Greatest Clubs

Liverpool FC

Matt Bougie

Cavendish Square
New York

Published in 2021 by Cavendish Square Publishing, LLC
243 5th Avenue, Suite 136, New York, NY 10016

First Edition

Library of Congress Cataloging-in-Publication Data

Names: Bougie, Matt, author.
Title: Liverpool FC / Matt Bougie.
Description: First edition. | New York, NY : Cavendish Square, 2021. | Series: Soccer's greatest clubs | Includes bibliographical references and index.
Identifiers: LCCN 2019042239 (print) | LCCN 2019042240 (ebook) | ISBN 9781502652805 (library binding) | ISBN 9781502652799 (paperback) | ISBN 9781502652812 (ebook)
Subjects: LCSH: Liverpool Football Club--History--Juvenile literature. | Soccer--England--Liverpool--History--Juvenile literature.
Classification: LCC GV943.6.L55 B68 2021 (print) | LCC GV943.6.L55 (ebook) | DDC 796.33409427/53--dc23
LC record available at https://lccn.loc.gov/2019042239
LC ebook record available at https://lccn.loc.gov/2019042240

Editor: Kristen Susienka
Copy Editor: Rebecca Rohan
Designer: Joe Parenteau

The photographs in this book are used by permission and through the courtesy of: Cover, p. 4 lev radin/Shutterstock.com; series art (badge) Onur Cem/Shutterstock.com; series art (field) comzeal images/Shutterstock.com; series art (soccer ball) FocusStocker/Shutterstock.com; series art (crowd silhouette) Nosyrevy/Shutterstock.com; p. 7 Hulton Archive/Getty Images; p. 8 PhotoLondonUK/Shutterstock.com; p. 10 Laurence Griffiths/Getty Images; p. 12 Empics/PA Images/Alamy Stock Photo; p. 14 History and Art Collection/Alamy Stock Photo; pp. 17, 21 Trinity Mirror/Mirrorpix/Alamy Stock Photo; p. 18 PBWPIX/Alamy Stock Photo; p. 20 Bridgeman Images; p. 23 Allsport/Getty Images; p. 24 Mirrorpix/Newscom; p. 25 Ian Hodgson/Reuters/Newscom; pp. 28, 30, 49 Allstar Picture Library/Alamy Stock Photo; p. 31 Peter Schatz/Alamy Stock Photo; p. 32 Carl Recine/Action Images via Reuters/Newscom; p. 35 MDI/Shutterstock.com; p. 36 David Edsam/Alamy Stock Photo; p. 41 Simon Dack/Telephoto Images/Alamy Stock Photo; p. 45 Jon Super/Action Images via Reuters/Newscom; p. 46 Cosminlftode/Shutterstock.com; p. 51 Jason Cairnduff/Action Images via Reuters/Newscom.

CPSIA compliance information: Batch #CS20CSQ: For further information contact Cavendish Square Publishing LLC, New York, New York, at 1-877-980-4450.

Printed in the United States of America

TABLE OF CONTENTS

Mohamed Salah (*left*) joined Liverpool in 2017 and soon became an exciting player for this famous club.

1 SOCCER AND LIVERPOOL FC

Soccer is the most popular sport in the world. It's played by people in nearly every country. Soccer involves a spherical ball and two teams. Each team tries to move the ball across a field and put it in a net at the other end of the field. Doing this is called scoring a goal. If a goal is scored, the team that scored is awarded one point. If no goal happens, no points are given.

Association football—the official name of soccer—was first organized in England in the 1850s. Today, it's played by 22 people at one time, with 11 players on each side. Players aren't allowed to touch the ball with their hands or arms, except for a player called the goalkeeper, or goalie. Each side has one goalie. The game is played in 45-minute halves. At the end of each half, a referee, or neutral official, can add more time. This is called stoppage time. It's based on how long general play had stopped during the game for things such as injuries. After the two halves are over and any stoppage time is played, the team with more points tied after all players have taken their shot at the goal, it goes into sudden death, which means that as soon as one team misses a goal, the other team can make their kick to win the game.

ENGLISH SOCCER

One of the world's most well-known soccer lineups, or leagues, is the English Football League (EFL). The EFL is composed of England's local teams that play each

A 1913 match between English teams Tottenham Hotspur and West Bromwich Albion shows that soccer matches were well attended, even more than 100 years ago.

Anfield is the home of Liverpool FC—one of the top teams in the EFL.

other for the chance to be the best team in the country. Some of the different competitions played in the EFL are the Community Shield, the EFL Cup, and the FA Cup. International competitions happen between the best teams from different countries. Big European tournaments are the Champions League and the Europa Cup.

The EFL has different levels, or divisions. Today, the top level is the Premier League, then the Championship League, then League One, and League Two. In the past, those divisions had different names. The idea is that every team in one division is similar in talent so that the matches are competitive. This also offers an incentive, or a good reason, for lower-level teams to try to win their way into higher levels. Playing in a higher-level division brings in more fans, earns the team more money, and helps the team attract better players. Still, lower-level teams also have great support, and matches are well attended.

One of the top teams in the EFL is Liverpool Football Club (FC). Begun in 1892, the club has been around almost as long as professional soccer has existed. In the past 127 years, the Reds, as they're nicknamed, have gone from a small team to a successful club with millions of fans around the world.

In terms of major trophies, Liverpool is the second–most decorated English soccer club as of late 2019, trailing their rivals Manchester United by a few titles.

FANS

Liverpool has tremendous fan support, not only in England but around the world. Their followers proudly wear their red jerseys at games and sing songs about the club.

One of the greatest traditions in all of English soccer is the singing of "You'll Never Walk Alone" as the Reds warm up on the field, or pitch. "You'll Never Walk Alone" was originally from the

Rodgers and Hammerstein musical *Carousel*, but it was covered by the band Gerry and the Pacemakers in 1963. The club adopted that version of the song the same year, and singing it in the stadium became a tradition. The words "You'll Never Walk Alone" were added to Liverpool's crest in 1992 as a celebration of the club's 100th anniversary, and many fans wear the initials Y.N.W.A. on merchandise.

These Liverpool fans are cheering on their club at their home stadium. They show their dedication to the team by holding up scarves with the team's name on them.

SPORT SHORT

The song "You'll Never Walk Alone" has become a popular song for other soccer clubs around the world, including Scotland's Celtic, Germany's Borussia Dortmund, the Netherlands' Feyenoord, and Japan's Tokyo FC.

INTO THE FUTURE

Even though Liverpool is a club rich in history, supporters and players are never content to live in the past. The club regularly brings in new and exciting players and pushes coaches to innovate and change the way they play. To be a Liverpool fan is to remember the team's past and be happy about its history of successes, but also to look toward the future and hope it continues being successful.

Liverpool founder John Houlding (*bottom row, seated, middle*) poses with an early squad.

2 THE ONGOING HISTORY OF LIVERPOOL FC

In the late 1800s, association football was just starting to get its bearings. A version of the game had been played for decades, but official rules were agreed upon in the 1800s, and in 1863, a soccer organization formed that would set out to manage the rules of the sport. This was called the Football Association, or FA. The Football Association still exists today and must approve all team changes or creations. This aspect became somewhat of a problem in the early history of Liverpool FC.

HOULDING, EVERTON, AND NEW BEGINNINGS

A man named John Houlding played an important role in founding Liverpool FC. Once, Houlding was Everton Football Club's president and owned a stadium called Anfield. Back then, Anfield was the home of Everton FC. Working with the Everton board, or group of directors, Houlding built a professional team that performed well against the other league teams.

However, John Houlding had some disagreements with his fellow board members about the direction of the club. After a particularly nasty argument involving the rent at Anfield, Everton FC moved across town to Goodison Park, leaving Anfield empty and leaving Houlding behind.

As the owner of a now-vacant field, Houlding decided to create his own team. To form a team quickly, Houlding went to Scotland and recruited many players, bringing them over to Liverpool to play. The Scottish players were eager to join and had a wealth of talent to contribute. As a result, this new team soon turned heads as strong competitors. However, their name was a bit of an obstacle at first. Houlding originally named it Everton FC and Athletic Grounds Limited, but the

Everton FC and Liverpool FC's histories are connected. This is the Everton FC team in 1887.

JOHN HOULDING

John Houlding was an English businessman and brewer who once served as the mayor of Liverpool in England. He was born in 1833 and died in 1902. Houlding founded the Liverpool Football Club.

As a businessman in the Liverpool community, Houlding was a member of the board for the Everton Football Club. While a member of the board, he worked out an agreement for a patch of land on Anfield Road, giving the Everton Football Club a place to play. He purchased the land in 1885 and began charging rent to the club. Houlding wanted the soccer club to buy Anfield from him, but they refused. This disagreement resulted in Everton moving to Goodison Park, leaving Houlding with an empty field.

Naturally, the next step was to create a new team to play in Anfield. Houlding founded Liverpool Football Club and quickly built a team to compete at a high level by recruiting players from Scotland. The Reds won their first title in 1901, just eight years after the club entered the league. Houlding died the next year, and players from both Liverpool FC and Everton FC carried his coffin, recognizing all he had done for their sport.

Football Association didn't like that since the name was too similar to Everton FC. Only after the name was changed to Liverpool Football Club was it accepted.

On June 3, 1892, the Liverpool Football Club was officially recognized by the city's Board of Trade, the department that helps regulate commerce. This meant that the club could start selling tickets, doing business, and building their fanbase. That same year, the team played its first game against Higher Walton, where Liverpool won 8–0.

Because they were a new team, the Reds started in the Lancashire League, a low-level league that accepted newly formed teams. The early years were good ones for the young club. They finished first in the Lancashire League in their first year, earning a promotion, or a move up, to the EFL's Second Division. Their first year in the Second Division was just as successful—they finished first and were at the top level of English soccer after two short years.

After the club was promoted, they would try for the league's top spot regularly. The team took First Division titles in 1906, 1922, 1923, and 1947. After winning in 1947, the team had some rough years and was eventually relegated, or moved down, to the Second Division in 1953.

SPORT SHORT

Liverpool's first uniforms were blue and white, instead of the familiar red outfit they wear now.

THE ICONIC COACH

After the team was relegated, Liverpool tended to hover around third or fourth place in the Second Division, not quite able to be promoted to the First Division. However, Liverpool's future as a top club was set in motion on December 1, 1959, when a man named Bill Shankly joined as coach.

As head coach of Liverpool, Bill Shankly helped bring the club success once again. He used a mix of smart coaching and hard work to do so.

Bill Shankly was originally from Scotland, but he'd had a long playing career in England, mostly for Preston North End, one of the founding teams in the English Football League. He played the position of midfielder, scoring 13 goals in 313 matches. After he retired from playing, he was immediately hired to coach. He managed four teams from 1949 to 1959 before receiving the offer to guide Liverpool.

EVERTON FOOTBALL CLUB

This statue of legendary Everton player William Ralph "Dixie" Dean stands outside the team's stadium, Goodison Park.

The Everton Football Club is Liverpool's oldest rival. As a founding member of the English Football League, Everton is one of the oldest professional soccer teams in England. They won their first league championship in their second year of existence. With royal blue shirts and white shorts, the team is nicknamed the Blues after their uniforms or the Toffees after a candy shop that was in Everton village.

Everton is a popular club. They have a strong international following and consistently make the top 10 for attendance at home matches. When Everton and Liverpool play each other, it's usually a sellout match, with fans able to stand next to each other with little incident. The pleasant interactions between the fans of these clubs has led this rivalry to be nicknamed "The Friendly Rivalry," and it's one of the few derbies, or local rival matches, where fans of opposing clubs are allowed to sit next to each other. Between 1894 and 2019, the teams have met 233 times, with Liverpool winning 93, Everton winning 66, and the two sides tying 74 times.

Shankly made it his mission not only to get the club promoted to the First Division, but also to keep the club successful by changing the way it worked. He set out to improve training facilities, realizing that better training and practice would lead to better results. He also created "the Boot Room," which was a small closet at Anfield where coaches would gather to talk about strategy, teams they would face, and how to improve the Liverpool team. By creating a group of coaches who worked and planned together, Shankly ensured that the club would continue to run smoothly if one coach left the team.

Shankly's strategies worked very well—so well, in fact, that the team got promoted after the 1961–1962 season. After eight years in the Second Division, Liverpool was finally back competing with England's top talent. They finished their first season back in the top league in eighth place but won the First Division title the following season, in 1964. This was the club's first major title since 1947. They followed up that win with a victory in the Football Association (FA) Cup tournament, and then another First Division title. Shankly decided to retire following the 1974 season, after winning one more division title in 1973 and another FA Cup in his last season with the team.

A RELUCTANT MANAGER ARRIVES

Shankly's planning set up the next 20 years of Liverpool dominance. Bob Paisley, one of the Boot Room coaches and a former Liverpool player, reluctantly but wholeheartedly took over for the 1975 season.

Coach Bob Paisley (*left*) celebrates Liverpool's first European Cup victory in 1977 with one of his players.

Liverpool finished as the runner-up in the First Division that year. The team did win a Charity Shield (now called Community Shield) during the season, however, making it three years in a row that the team brought home a major award. Paisley coached the team for nine seasons and won six League Championships, three League Cups, three European Cups, and six Charity Shields. Many talented players found success also during Paisley's reign, including Kenny Dalglish, Graeme Souness, and Ian Rush.

Paisley retired in 1983 after spending 44 years with the team as a player, assistant, and head coach. However, Liverpool allegiance ran deep in Paisley, and he couldn't step away completely. He acted as an informal advisor to later manager Kenny Dalglish and then became a team director until 1992, when he retired due to failing health. He died in 1996.

A QUIET LEADER IN AN IMPOSSIBLE SITUATION

After Paisley, Joe Fagan, another member of the Boot Room brigade, took over. He would only coach for two years, however. In that short time, he brought home three trophies in his first year. His second year ended not only in disappointment, but also in tragedy. Besides the team not taking home any hardware, or trophies, in 1985, 39 people, mostly fans of the Italian Juventus club, were killed in Heysel Stadium in Brussels during the European Cup finals.

The game was between Juventus and Liverpool. Its winner would be a European champion. Fans came from all over the world. English fans and Juventus fans were separated, but a neutral fan area was set up next to the Liverpool section. Juventus fans—including

This image shows the aftermath of the Heysel disaster in 1985.

families—filled the neutral area. About an hour before the game started, English fans began to come to the neutral section through a gap in a fence, angered by the Juventus fans being there. More and more Liverpool fans arrived, and Juventus fans panicked. Many were crushed against a concrete wall. Some were able to escape onto the field, but many more were badly injured or killed in the chaos. Fourteen Liverpool fans were put in jail for these events, and all English clubs faced a five-year ban from UEFA matches. (UEFA stands for Union of European Football Associations. It's a governing body for international soccer games and clubs.) Liverpool faced a six-year ban from UEFA matches.

With this shadow hanging over the club, Fagan retired at the end of the season. As a manager, Fagan never craved the spotlight. After retiring, he returned to private life, offering advice to managers when asked but staying out of the limelight. Much like he did as an assistant coach, Fagan preferred to work hard in the background, helping where he could. His quiet dedication and work ethic were key factors in establishing Liverpool's dominance while Shankly and Paisley were the head coaches. Joe Fagan died in 2001 at the age of 80.

"KING KENNY" DALGLISH

Kenny Dalglish started his soccer career in Scotland before coming to Liverpool in 1977 as a player. He's thought to be one of the best forwards, or strikers, in English soccer history. Because he played and managed

Kenny Dalglish (*center*) holds off Kevin Moran (*right*) of Manchester United during the English League Cup final in 1983. Dalglish is a beloved former Liverpool player and coach.

so well, and was so beloved by Liverpool fans, they nicknamed him "King of the Kop" or "King Kenny."

After Fagan retired in 1985, Dalglish took over the manager role while still playing with the team, becoming what's called a player-manager. Dalglish had a lot of success with the team. He remains a fan favorite today, not only because he helped bring home title after title, but also because the style of soccer he played and coached was entertaining and fun to watch.

However, Dalglish also dealt with a difficult time in Liverpool history when the Hillsborough disaster

SPORT SHORT

A nickname for one of the seating areas in Anfield is the Kop. It honors Liverpudlians, or Liverpool citizens, who died during the Boer War (1899–1902).

Fans climbed the walls of Hillsborough Stadium to avoid being crushed in the press of bodies.

occurred on April 15, 1989. He was coach of the club and at Hillsborough Stadium the day tragedy struck right before an FA Cup semifinal match between Liverpool and Nottingham Forest. Ninety-six fans died, crushed to death near the field because of poor crowd management.

Dalglish attended as many of the funerals as he could and worked hard to support the families of the victims. He handled a terrible tragedy with poise and dignity, never forgetting the people who suffered. The fans loved him for that. In 2017, the club honored King Kenny by renaming one of their stands after him.

A LONG HISTORY OF RIVALRIES

Liverpool has rivals throughout the Premier League—the current name for the top level of English soccer—but there are a few clubs that go beyond a normal rivalry and become about something more. Liverpool's two biggest rivals are Everton and Manchester United. The rivalry with Everton is the longest-running rivalry in top-level soccer, starting in 1894. When the two clubs meet, it's called the Merseyside derby, named after Merseyside County, where both teams play.

Even though Liverpool shares a city with Everton, most Liverpool fans don't consider the crosstown

Matches between Liverpool and Manchester United can get quite heated. Here, Manchester United goalkeeper Massimo Taibi (*left*) tries to stop a goal from Liverpool during a game in 1999.

team their biggest rivals. The rivalry with Manchester United hasn't been as friendly as the one with Everton. While Liverpool and Manchester United don't share a city, they do share a similar level of success. Their rivalry started in the industrial era due to their close proximity—they're 34 miles (55 kilometers) apart—and competing companies in similar industries. Essentially, the cities were competing with each other, and that spilled over into soccer. Today, the competitive rivalry continues, especially in soccer.

While sometimes tense, the scenes on the field are entertaining for both sides. When the two clubs meet, fans will chant songs about their team or call each other names. Sometimes the names aren't nice, though. If name-calling reaches an extreme, fans will be punished. Both teams appreciate their fans' enthusiasm, but they try to make the rivalry more about the game on the field than anything else. They take name-calling and more violent acts seriously.

For Liverpool faithful, a Manchester United loss is *almost* as good as a Liverpool win—and a win against Manchester United is something to be remembered and treasured. Because this rivalry is so intense, there is an unspoken agreement that a Manchester United player should never join Liverpool and a Liverpool player should never join Manchester United.

In rare times when a player does switch sides, returning to his former team's stadium is always an ordeal. One of the last players to play for both Liverpool and Manchester United was Michael Owen. He was a star for Liverpool between 1996 and 2004.

After an excellent career with Liverpool, Owen joined Real Madrid, a soccer team in Spain. Real Madrid transferred, or moved, him to Newcastle United in England, where he played for three years. After Newcastle was relegated, Owen could join whatever team he wanted, and in 2009, he agreed to play with Manchester United. Liverpool fans who once loved watching him play saw this as an ultimate betrayal and turned on him, even though he had played for two different clubs before signing with Manchester United.

While Liverpool enjoyed its greatest successes in the 1970s and 1980s, Manchester United saw two decades of success starting in the 1990s and continuing into the 2000s. When Liverpool was very successful, Manchester United was experiencing some down years and seemed unable to make the jump to being a top team. When Manchester United was winning title after title in the 1990s, Liverpool was finishing well below expectations. Both teams having such a long history of success only fueled the rivalry. Overall, Manchester United has the edge in head-to-head matchups as well as major awards, but Liverpool only needs a few great seasons to turn the tide.

Liverpool player Steven Gerrard lifts the European Cup after winning in Istanbul in 2005.

3 A HISTORY OF SUCCESS

The 20th and 21st centuries brought a mix of success and disappointment for Liverpool. In addition to their dominant run in the 1970s and 1980s, Liverpool enjoyed some impressive seasons in the late 1990s and 2000s.

While Liverpool hasn't captured a Premier League Championship since the 1989–1990 season, they won the Champions League in 2004–2005, along with FA Cups in 1999–2000 and in 2004–2005. During this streak, Steven Gerrard was the star player for Liverpool. He was a fan favorite not only because he was born just outside Liverpool, but he also grew up rooting for the team, was an incredibly talented player, and stayed with the club for 17 years. Gerrard was a model of consistency, appearing in 710 matches and scoring 186 goals in his club career.

GERRARD'S MAGIC

Gerrard also helped during big matches. During the 2004–2005 Champions League final against an Italian team called AC Milan, which was played at the

Steven Gerrard (*center*) celebrates the Champions League victory against AC Milan in 2005.

Ataturk Olympic Stadium in Istanbul, Liverpool was losing 3–0 at halftime. It looked like AC Milan would win the game. Instead of giving up, Liverpool staged an incredible comeback with Gerrard scoring the first goal after the half. The game went into extra time and then penalty kicks. In the end, Liverpool won the match—and the European Cup. People remember this as one of the most exciting matches in Champions League history. For his part, Steven Gerrard would be

SPORT SHORT

Between 1975 and 1991, Liverpool finished in either first or second place in the First Division 18 out of 19 seasons.

LIVERPOOL FC WOMEN

Liverpool FC Women's Rhiannon Roberts (*left*) battles Bayern Munich's Melanie Leupolz (*right*) in a non-competitive match in 2018.

The history of the Liverpool FC Women isn't as long as that of the men's club, but it has just as much pride. First named the Newton Ladies, the team began in 1989. That year, they won the Lancashire International tournament and made it to the finals in both Division One and Division Two. In 1995, the Newton Ladies became the Liverpool FC Ladies and reached the Women's FA Cup final, narrowly losing. The team won their first title in 2013 and a second in 2014, and they remain among the best teams in Women's Premier League Football.

The team plays in Prenton Park in Birkenhead with a stadium able to hold 16,000 people. The team is very active in the soccer community, offering development leagues where talented young female players can receive top-rate instruction. By mentoring young women, Liverpool can continue to have a competitive team as well as increase interest in and support for the sport among young women.

remembered as a hero in Liverpool, and people would call that match the Miracle of Istanbul.

Besides winning the Miracle of Istanbul, Liverpool struggled to take home trophies after their run of dominance in the 1980s, but they came close many times. In the 21st century, they finished as runners-up for the FA Cup in 2012 and runners-up in the Champions League in 2017–2018. The club also came in second in the Premier League in 2013–2014 as well as in 2018–2019, losing to Manchester City by a single point. It looked as though Liverpool would end the 2018–2019 season without a major victory again, but a furious comeback in a game against AC Milan won the team its first Champions League title since the Miracle of Istanbul.

Goalie Alisson Becker thanks fans after winning the Golden Glove award in 2019.

AWARDS TODAY

Although team trophies have been tougher to win in recent seasons, individual players have been recognized by the Premier League. In 2019, Liverpool player Virgil van Dijk won the Premier League Player of the Season award for his hard work during the 2018–2019 run. Also in that season, Alisson Becker (known just as Alisson) won the Golden Glove award, highlighting his achievement as the goalkeeper with the least amount of goals scored on him during the season. Mohamed Salah and Sadio Mané won the Golden Boot award (Salah in 2017–2018 and 2018–2019 and Mané in 2018–2019). This award recognizes players who score the most goals during a season. Brendan Rodgers, manager of Liverpool from 2012 to 2015, won the Manager of the Year title in 2014. It's clear that Liverpool is determed to make their mark in soccer, with or without trophies.

MANAGERS MAKE A DIFFERENCE

Like most teams, Liverpool has had a history of both good and bad managers. In the 1990s and 2000s, when the club struggled to succeed for a time, Liverpool had a string of managers who didn't last long. Because of the lack of trophies and consistency, the club's owners looked to make a more reliable and long-term hire in the 2010s. Brendan Rodgers joined in 2012. It was hoped he would help reshape the club, but Liverpool finished in sixth place in the 2014–2015 season, prompting Rodgers to leave the club in the 2015–2016 season. Shortly following Rodgers's dismissal, Liverpool hired a new manager who they hoped would be able to help them reclaim a Premier League title, which they hadn't won since 1990–1991. Jürgen Klopp was this coach, and the club brought him in to install a new German strategy called *Gegenpressing*.

SPORT SHORT

Since being promoted to the top division in 1956, Liverpool has not finished lower than eighth in the Premier League.

THE LFC FOUNDATION

Being one of the wealthiest sports clubs in the world, Liverpool FC uses its resources and visibility to promote numerous charitable causes. The LFC Foundation, the official charity of the club, sponsors numerous events and causes. The foundation runs community sessions for children to play sports, interact with each other, and experience things that they might not otherwise be able to due to physical disabilities. It also offers activities for seniors, runs food drives for families in need, and does general community outreach.

The LFC Foundation also works with LGBTQ+ organizations as well as minority organizations to create an inclusive environment. The goal of the foundation is to take the passion that surrounds the club and use it to improve the lives of everyone in the community.

Gegenpressing relies on speed, stamina, and making quick decisions instead of a more methodical and conservative play style. It requires players to try to quickly win back the ball after losing possession. Approaches include hard tackles, quick passes, and swarming defenders.

Once Klopp installed this strategy, spectators quickly began to enjoy it. It seems to work too! In the 2018–2019 season, Liverpool scored often, even though the aggressiveness on defense sometimes allowed for opponents to sneak through and score. Making this strategy work consistently requires a lot of practicing and excellent communication between the players and coaches, as well as incredible stamina because players are running long distances constantly. It also requires a good goalkeeper and defenders.

Not only has this hyperaggressive style led to more goals for Liverpool, but it's also very fun to watch. The ball moves constantly, and Liverpool defenders are often able to steal the ball and make a break for the goal. Fans love watching how quickly the players can turn a defensive moment into a staggering counterattack ending in an exciting goal. Hiring Jürgen Klopp and adding more talented players to the team has Liverpool fans excited for the future.

Coach Jürgen Klopp holds the European Cup trophy in celebration after Liverpool won the Champions League in 2019.

Liverpool fans cheer on their team during a game in 2004.

4

FACING SOCIETAL AND SPORT ISSUES

As with any sports team, there are challenges facing Liverpool outside of the game. The challenges have changed over the years, but any negative events can upset a fan's enjoyment of the game or even endanger spectators. Liverpool has worked hard to tackle problems and make the game fun for everyone, but the team still has work to do, as does the entire league. Key issues affecting the sport today are overexcited fans, match-fixing, racism, and violence.

HOOLIGANISM

In the 1970s, hooliganism threatened to bring the sport of soccer down within England. Hooliganism is a kind of organized violence that happens between some soccer fans, and in the 1970s, the violence was so prevalent that people considered shutting down the league to prevent it. English fans were known around the world for their disruptive behavior.

Fan groups would travel to away games and cause trouble with anyone who got in their way—this could be other similar groups or innocent bystanders. Some

FENWAY SPORTS GROUP AND BUYING LIVERPOOL

In 2010, Liverpool FC almost went bankrupt. The club was put up for sale to help pay off debts. On October 15, 2010, the Fenway Sports Group purchased the team, along with Anfield, for $560 million.

The Fenway Sports Group is an organization that specializes in sports, marketing, and broadcasting. It also owns the Boston Red Sox and their stadium Fenway Park in the United States, giving Liverpool an interesting connection to one of America's oldest cities. On occasion, Liverpool will travel to the United States to play a preseason game at Fenway Park. The last time they did this was in July 2019, right before the start of the 2019–2020 season. A crowd of over 35,000 attended.

of these groups just liked the chaos that happened in these large-scale fights, but some used the excitement and disorganization of soccer games to target specific people. It took a concentrated effort from police as well as clubs to create lists of known hooligans and prevent them from entering stadiums. Stronger law enforcement presence on match days also helped slow the violence down. Today, organized groups still seek out certain bars or hangouts to try to provoke opposing fans. Overall, though, any violence that does happen is usually less organized than it once was.

While incidents at matches are rare today, they do still happen. For example, during a match between Aston Villa and Birmingham in 2019, a fan ran onto the field and punched midfielder Jack Grealish in the back of the head. Luckily, Grealish wasn't seriously hurt and went on to score the winning goal, but it was a reminder that there is still work to be done to secure the safety of players and fans who participate in or attend matches.

During the 2019 season, Liverpool dealt with examples of hooliganism leading up to international matches. In 2019, Liverpool was set to play Barcelona during the Champions League. Several Liverpool fans in Barcelona were filmed pushing unsuspecting people into fountains and then taunting them as they emerged soaking wet. Liverpool didn't approve of the acts, and the club's CEO asked all Liverpool fans to act graciously and show the city and its people the respect they deserved. Clubs, police, and other fans need to make sure that hooligans or other troublemakers don't become the face of the club, and they need to work to stop their behavior. Soccer is a sport enjoyed by millions of people across the world, and violence has no place in the experience.

SPORT SHORT

Liverpool first wore their all-red uniforms in 1964 in an effort to appear more intimidating. From then on, they became known as the Reds.

MATCH-FIXING

Match-fixing has plagued European soccer for decades and continues in the 21st century. Liverpool's early match-fixing involvement started in 1915. In fact, they were joined in the rigging by rivals Manchester United. Toward the end of the 1915–1916 season, both Liverpool and Manchester United were near the bottom of the league. To avoid relegation, a third party approached several players on both sides to try to convince them to let Manchester United win a match 2–0, allowing the team to avoid relegation. The players would also be able to place wagers, or bets, on the outcome, meaning that they would be able to collect quite a lot of money for correct guesses.

Because World War I had begun in 1914 and players were already starting to head off to fight, there was a great incentive for the players to participate in the fix. They didn't know if there would be organized soccer the following season because of the war, and they also didn't know if they'd be called to serve. Authorities got suspicious, and after the match, four Liverpool players and three Manchester United players received lifetime bans for their part in the fix. After the war, most players had their bans lifted in recognition of their war effort.

Liverpool has had a clean slate after that, but some reported match-fixing has been rumored to involve their opponents in the recent past. In 2009, one game they played against Hungarian team Debrecen was investigated for match-fixing, and some Debrecen players were penalized. In 2018, another team in the Champions League group that Liverpool played in was investigated for match-fixing.

RACISM

Throughout history, racism and other kinds of prejudice have been a problem in professional soccer just as they've been a problem within society as a whole. Players who are races other than white or who have different religious backgrounds are often targets of abuse from fans—and sometimes even from other players.

In recent years, the Premier League, as well as individual teams, has taken steps to lessen racism in the sport. Organizations like Kick It Out offer education and diversity training for players. They also use apps and websites to note incidents of racism so individual cases can be addressed and investigated. If a fan is treating others disrespectfully, other fans can report them, and the fan can be removed from the game and possibly banned from games in the future. Threats like these can make a fan think twice before using racist language.

The No Room for Racism Campaign is a joint effort between all Premier League teams to remove racism from the game of soccer. Here, students hold up a banner advertising the project before a game in 2019.

HILLSBOROUGH

One of the most tragic events for Liverpool on the field happened on April 15, 1989. At a game between Liverpool and Nottingham Forest, 96 people were killed at Hillsborough Stadium in Sheffield, England.

The disaster occurred right before kickoff when police opened a gate that allowed more Liverpool fans into an already overcrowded area. Back then, many fans stood in sections called pens or terraces at a stadium, rather than sit down in assigned seats. That day, the people at the back of the pen didn't know that there was no more room at the front, and the people at the front were pushed into a fence that separated the pen from the field. With nowhere to go and pressure piling on from the back of the crowd, people were crushed. Almost 100 were pressed to death and more than 700 were injured.

Instantly following the tragedy, officials blamed the fans. This was easily believed, since at that time English fans had a reputation for hooliganism. However, later, an official report about the tragedy found that the main cause of the crush was a failure of the police to properly control the situation and direct people into uncrowded side pens. Authorities concluded all of the deaths to be accidental, and no criminal charges were brought against anyone. Families of the victims were very angry, since they hoped the officers would be punished more harshly.

For decades, Liverpool FC and its fans didn't believe the fans in the area were causing trouble that day and knew they didn't deserve to be blamed. They tried for years to get the case reopened. After many campaigns and protests, a second look into the Hillsborough disaster, as it's called, was opened in 2012. Hearings began in 2014. In April 2016, 27 years after the tragedy, a jury gave a verdict, or official decision, of unlawful killing, officially stating that the fans at the stadium that day were blameless.

In the immediate aftermath of Hillsborough, the entire soccer community began improving the safety conditions at all stadiums. Standing terraces were taken away from all stadiums, and every spectator would have a seat. This prevented overselling the match and allowed for a safer flow of people into an area. Stadiums also put up gates that could be opened in case of an emergency, making it easier for people to escape if there was a problem. Through this great loss, a greater sense of safety across professional soccer emerged.

SPORT SHORT

Fans who sit in the Kop section of the stadium are referred to as "Koppites," and they're known as being some of the most loyal supporters of Liverpool.

In March 2019, the Premier League launched its No Room for Racism campaign, focused on showing that racism wouldn't be tolerated within stadiums. This campaign included advertising and supporting diversity initiatives, such as the Black and Ethnic Minority Coach Initiative, which encourages minority populations and women to enter coaching. The league has also started punishing players and fans who act in racist ways or use vulgar language, suspending players from league matches or charging fines. Some spectators have been banned from attending matches for their actions.

Some people criticized these approaches, saying that the punishments aren't handed out effectively, with some people escaping punishment. Others say that these initiatives don't do enough to address the underlying problem. However, fans and players hope that, by making these changes and continuing efforts to support diversity, they will help eliminate racism in the game.

MOVING FORWARD

Individual clubs have a responsibility to police their own players and fans, making sure that everyone who attends a match is safe and treated with respect.

Liverpool benefits from having players who stand up to racism on and off the field.

During the 2018–2019 season, there was a renewed effort to remove racism from soccer, especially after Napoli defender Kalidou Koulibaly was subjected to terrible racist chants during a match with Inter Milan, and there were so many fans chanting that they could not be effectively removed from the game. Instead, Koulibaly had to endure the taunting for his entire time on the field. Liverpool players Mohamed Salah, an Egyptian native, and Sadio Mané, a native of Senegal, issued statements of support for Koulibaly, showing they understood how difficult it is for a player to keep his mind on the match when people are chanting behind him. Many other players offered their support as well, including soccer superstar Cristiano Ronaldo and Inter Milan captain Mauro Icardi. Recognizing that removing racism from soccer has to be a joint effort across teams, these players are helping to make soccer stadiums more inclusive places and show that soccer is for everyone.

Napoli's Kalidou Koulibaly (*right*) challenges Liverpool's James Milner (*left*) during a match in 2018.

Mohamed Salah (*right*) celebrates after making a penalty shot during the 2018–2019 UEFA Champions League final.

5 CURRENT AND FUTURE SUCCESSES

It would be easy for Liverpool FC to rest on past successes and point to them as signs of greatness. That won't comfort fans, though, who want the team to win more trophies and awards and stay successful today. Liverpool's legacy is ongoing and is enriched with every goal, every player signing, and every new fan. The Reds plan to look toward the future and, as always, aim to build a team that will compete at the highest level and entertain fans while they do it.

A SEASON IN REVIEW

In 2018–2019, Liverpool had a fantastic season. They scored more points in the Premier League than they ever had before, with a total of 97. In fact, they only lost one match the entire year. They did tie seven times, and unfortunately, Manchester City finished with 98 points, leaving Liverpool with a second-place finish. However, 97 points was the highest total points for a second-place finish in Premier League history. Still, it

SPORT SHORT

Liverpool celebrated its 125th anniversary in 2017. The team marked the occasion with various special events and merchandise throughout the year.

did come as a disappointment for the fans, who hoped this would be the year the team ended their Premier League drought.

Liverpool also qualified to play in the Champions League during the 2018–2019 season. The team played well, advancing to the semifinals where they faced Barcelona, a club from Spain. In the first leg (or game), Barcelona beat Liverpool badly, winning 3–0. Most people thought that the results were decided. Coming back from a 0–3 match is very difficult and doesn't tend to happen. Instead of giving up, though, Liverpool went into the second leg of the tournament and played aggressively. Liverpool scored 4 goals in the second leg, stunning Barcelona and sending Liverpool to the finals on a 4–3 aggregate score.

In the finals, Liverpool faced Tottenham Hotspur, another English club. Liverpool took an early lead on a penalty kick and never looked back. They beat Tottenham 2–0, winning the Champions League for the sixth time in club history. Fans were excited to see Liverpool bring home a major award for the first time in almost 15 years.

As of late 2019, the team was in first place in the Premier League for the 2019–2020 season.

INDIVIDUAL ACCOMPLISHMENTS

In terms of players, Liverpool has also excelled in the 2010s. Such greats as Luis Suárez, Mohamed Salah, and Sadio Mané appeared regularly on the top of the playing deck.

In 2018–2019, the club saw great production from team members like Salah and Mané in particular. Salah scored 22 goals in Premier League play. The Egyptian national also had one of the most spectacular goals in an April 14, 2019, match against Chelsea. The ball

Liverpool players celebrate during the 2019 Champions League final against Tottenham Hotspur.

zoomed toward the net like a laser, settling into the top corner of the goal past the diving goalkeeper. Mané also had a marvelous season, keeping Liverpool in contention when Salah was unable to score. The Senegal native also ended with 22 league goals, matching his teammate. Both players won a Golden Boot award for their efforts.

Virgil van Dijk transferred to the team during the 2017–2018 season and quickly showed his ability to defend against some of the toughest attackers. He was nominated as one of the six Players of the Year for 2018–2019 and won the award for his defensive play, making it the second year in a row that a Liverpool player was given this honor. Mohamed Salah won it in 2017–2018 with his spectacular offense.

TAKING LIVERPOOL INTO THE FUTURE

Liverpool supporters have to be happy with the path the team has been following in recent years. Jürgen Klopp's coaching strategy and playing suggestions make for very entertaining soccer. With his help, the team performed extraordinarily well in 2018–2019. It's not just the managing that matters, though. Liverpool has some of the most exciting players in the game today—such as Salah, Mané, van Dijk, and Roberto Firmino. Not only is the team already good, but they also are poised to bring in more players and compete at an even higher level.

To help keep the team performing at a high level for years to come, Liverpool has the Liverpool Academy

The Liverpool Under-18 youth team celebrates winning the FA Youth Cup in 2019.

and youth training teams. The Academy program helps train and develop young players who show talent now and will ideally improve as they get older and start contributing to the top club. Several high-level players, including Trent Alexander-Arnold and Steven Gerrard, graduated from the Academy and went on to become excellent players for Liverpool.

A strong youth program, along with good coaching and good training, has the team ready to continue competing at the highest level over the years to come. As the current top players start getting older, begin to retire, or move on to different teams, these new players will join the club.

New talent also often comes from youth teams. Liverpool and many other teams have underage groups, including Under-17s and Under-23s. Members of the Under-23 squad are sometimes called to be substitutes for the professional Liverpool team if an injury happens or a player needs to rest. This squad plays against other Under-23 squads to develop their talents.

As they continue to develop, keep an eye out for some promising young players on Liverpool's professional and Under-23 teams. Joe Gomez is a young defender who joined Liverpool in 2015 at the age of 18. No doubt he will continue to be an outstanding player for the club. Rhian Brewster was born in 2000 and had 20 goals in 23 appearances in the Under-17 League during the 2016–2017 season. He was a crucial player in the Under-23 team's push for the Premier League Cup in 2019–2020. His exciting offensive play also gives Liverpool supporters a lot to look forward to in the coming years.

The future looks good for this historic club. It's a good time to be a supporter of the Liverpool Reds!

CHRONOLOGY

1892 Liverpool Football Club is formed.

1901 Liverpool wins its first title, topping the First Division.

1947 Liverpool wins the first title after the end of World War II, beating out Manchester United by a single point.

1954 After losing to Cardiff City (Wales), Liverpool is demoted to the Second Division.

1959 Bill Shankly signs on to be the coach of Liverpool FC.

1962 The Reds are promoted to the top division—and haven't been relegated since.

1964 Liverpool FC players march out in a completely red uniform, marking the start of a new tradition.

1965 Liverpool wins its first FA Cup.

1972 Liverpool kicks off its first season of top-level dominance, starting a run where the club finished in first or second place in the EFL for 18 out of 19 seasons.

1973 Liverpool wins their first European Cup.

1985 The Heysel Stadium disaster occurs. Thirty-nine fans lose their lives during the European Cup final.

1989 Ninety-six fans die in the Hillsborough disaster.

1990 Liverpool wins its 18th Premier League title.

1994 The Kop converts from standing to seated as a direct response to the Hillsborough disaster.

2005 Steven Gerrard kicks off a flurry of Liverpool scoring against AC Milan, and Liverpool goes on to win the Champions League title on penalty kicks.

2012 Brendan Rodgers joins as manager of Liverpool from Swansea FC.

2015 Brendan Rodgers leaves the club, and Jürgen Klopp becomes manager soon after.

2017 Liverpool celebrates its 125th year of existence.

2019 Liverpool wins the Champions League.

GLOSSARY

aggregate The number of points across two legs played between teams (the legs are one home game and one away game).

board A group of businesspeople who meet to make decisions about an organization or company.

Champions League A tournament-style league where the top teams in Europe play each other until one winner emerges.

commerce Business.

cover A recording of a song performed by a band or artist other than the original.

crest A logo or badge on a sports jersey, usually appearing inside a circle on the front of the jersey.

derby A match between local rivals. They may be in the same city or same part of the country.

extra time A period of time in a game that is played after normal playing time has ended if no winner is determined.

FA Cup An annual knockout tournament played in England. This tournament not only includes professional teams, but can also include local and lower-level teams.

fanbase A group of fans.

Gegenpressing A soccer strategy where players try to win back the ball after losing possession instead of regrouping and setting up a defense.

halftime The period after the first 45 minutes of a soccer game is played when the teams take a break in their locker room to rest and discuss strategy.

hooligans Semiorganized gangs that follow a specific team and commit various crimes.

incentive Motivation.

neutral Not supporting a specific team.

pitch A soccer field.

poise The ability to carry oneself well and in a balanced manner.

Premier League The top division in English football; it replaced the "First Division" in 1992.

promote To move a team up from one league to another.

relegate To drop a soccer team from one division to the next lower division as a result of not having enough points to stay in the division at the end of a season.

transfer To trade a player directly between teams.

vacant Empty.

vulgar Tasteless and rude.

work ethic The will to work hard to achieve goals.

FURTHER INFORMATION

BOOKS

Anderson, Jeff, and Stephen Done. *The Official Liverpool FC Illustrated Encyclopedia*. London, UK: Carlton, 2016.

Bandy, James. *The Ultimate Guide to the Premier League*. Edinburgh, UK: Grange Communications Ltd, 2018.

Besley, Adrian. *Mohamed Salah: The Ultimate Fan Book*. London, UK: Carlton, 2018.

Platt, Mark. *Official Liverpool FC Annual 2019*. Edinburgh, UK: Grange Communications Ltd, 2018.

Williams, John. *Red Men: Liverpool Football Club: The Biography*. Edinburgh, UK: Mainstream, 2011.

WEBSITES

15 Weird and Wonderful Facts about Liverpool FC

anfieldindex.com/36402/15-weird-and-wonderful-facts-about-liverpool-f-c.html

At this website, you'll find 15 fun facts about Liverpool FC.

Kop Kids

www.liverpoolfc.com/kopkids

This website is full of activities, videos, and pictures put out by the official team website.

Our Story: Celebrating 127 Years of the Liverpool Way

www.liverpoolfc.com/history

Here you will find a detailed history of the club highlighting heroes and historic events.

This Is Anfield

www.thisisanfield.com

This fan site features quizzes, interviews, and match reports.

VIDEOS

Liverpool's Legendary Manager Bill Shankly and the Boot Room

www.youtube.com/watch?v=Et-RW1OZ46E

This video gives background information on Bill Shankly and his Boot Room coaches.

Milan 3–3 Liverpool: UCL 2005 Final Flashback

www.youtube.com/watch?v=3OQToElxke4

This video recaps Liverpool's stunning come-from-behind Champions League final match against AC Milan in Istanbul.

What Happened at Hillsborough?

www.youtube.com/watch?v=MNS26Oj9B4o

This BBC examination provides insight into the tragedy at Hillsborough.

SELECTED BIBLIOGRAPHY

Bandy, James. *The Ultimate Guide to the Premier League.* Edinburgh, UK: Grange Communications Ltd, 2018.

CNN Library. "Hillsborough Stadium Disaster Fast Facts." CNN, April 2, 2019. www.cnn.com/2016/04/25/world/hillsborough-disaster-fast-facts/index.html.

"Hillsborough Disaster: From Tragedy to Truth." BBC News. Accessed August 24, 2019. www.bbc.com/timelines/zpdc7hv.

"International Academy." Liverpool FC. soccerschools.liverpoolfc.com/.

"LFC History." LFCHistory.net. www.lfchistory.net.

"Liverpool FC Official Site." Liverpool FC. www.liverpoolfc.com.

Matchett, Karl. "Liverpool's Champions League Group Hit by Match-Fixing Investigation." This Is Anfield. www.thisisanfield.com/2018/10/liverpools-champions-league-group-hit-by-match-fixing-investigation.

"Match-Fixing: Debrecen Confirm Liverpool Investigation." BBC Sport, February 5, 2013. https://www.bbc.com/sport/football/21335331.

"1989: Football Fans Crushed at Hillsborough." BBC News. BBC, April 15, 1989. news.bbc.co.uk/onthisday/hi/dates/stories/april/15/newsid_2491000/2491195.stm.

Peace, David. *Red or Dead: A Novel.* Brooklyn, NY: Melville House, 2015.

Pead, Brian. *Liverpool: A Complete Record 1892–1986.* Derby, England, UK: Breedon Books, 1986.

Platt, Mark. *The Official Liverpool FC Annual 2019*. Edinburgh, UK: Grange Communications Ltd, 2018.

Smith, Rory. "Liverpool and Everton No Longer Play the 'Friendly Derby' as Fans Become More Vitriolic." *Telegraph*, January 24, 2009. www.telegraph.co.uk/sport/football/teams/liverpool/4333250/Liverpool-and-Everton-no-longer-play-the-friendly-derby-as-fans-become-more-vitriolic-Football.html.

Williams, John. *Red Men: Liverpool Football Club: The Biography*. Edinburgh, UK: Mainstream, 2011.

INDEX

ABOUT THE AUTHOR

Matt Bougie is writer and marketer from Friendship, Wisconsin, currently living in Milwaukee, Wisconsin. He is the author of several books, including *Tech in the Trenches: Strategic Inventions of the Cold War* and *American Legends and Folktales: The Bell Witch: Ghost of Tennessee*. Bougie enjoys reading and writing, especially about history, sports, and technology.